Child Abuse

Child Abuse

Were You Abused As A Child?

Oliver JR Cooper

Also By Oliver JR Cooper

A Dialogue With The Heart – Part One: A Collection Of Poems And Dialogues From The Heart

Trapped Emotions – How Are They Affecting Your Life?

Childhood – Is Your Childhood Sabotaging Your Life?

A Dialogue With The Heart – Part Two: A Collection Of Poems And Dialogues From The Heart

Toxic Shame – Is It Defining Your Life?

Abandonment – Is The Fear Of Abandonment Controlling Your Life?

Note to Readers

That which is contained within this book is based upon my own experiences, research and views up until the point of publication. It is not to be taken as the truth or the only viable viewpoint. It is not intended to diagnose or cure any disease.

This book is dedicated to Molly James. Thank you for being there in the beginning and for the faith you showed in me.

Child Abuse – Were You Abused As A Child?

Edited By – Jessica Coleman

© 2015 Oliver JR Cooper

All rights reserved worldwide. No part of this publication may be copied, modified, reproduced, or translated in any form or by any means, electronic, mechanical, recoding, or otherwise, without permission from Oliver JR Cooper.

ISBN-13: 978-1518693946
ISBN-10: 1518693946

For information, please contact:

www.oliverjrcooper.co.uk

Contents

Introduction
Words from the Author... 1

Why has Child Abuse Gone On for So Long? 5

Chapter One – In the Beginning
Why are Children Abused? 13

Why Would a Primary Caregiver be Abusive?....... 17

Why Would a Caregiver be Controlling? 21

Chapter Two – Generational Abuse
Why Does Abuse get Passed on?.......................... 29

Why Does Neglect get Passed on?....................... 35

Chapter Three – Denial
Do You Deny what Happened?.............................. 43

Do They Deny what Happened? 47

Do Other People Deny that You Were Abused? ... 51

Do You Idealise your Caregivers?......................... 55

Chapter Four – The Consequences

Do You Feel like there is Something Wrong with You? 61

What are the Effects of Having a Caregiver who was Verbally Abusive? 63

What are the Effects of Having a Primary Caregiver who was Emotionally Unavailable? 67

What are the Effects of Being Invalidated as a Child? 71

Is Having Boundary Problems Normal? 75

Do You Tolerate Unhealthy Relationships? 79

Chapter Five – Moving Forward

Do You Need to Forgive Them? 87

Is it Important to be Angry about what Happened? 91

Is Feeling Safe an Important Part of Healing? 95

Is Being Validated an Important Part of Healing? .. 99

Is Crying an important Part of Healing from Abuse? 103

Acknowledgments 109

About the Author 111

Introduction

Words from the Author

During the early years of someone's life, they look towards their caregivers to protect them, and through living in an environment that is secure, it counterbalances what takes place in the outside world.

The consistency (among other things) that they experience allows them to grow, and they can enjoy this time in their lives. When this happens, there is a strong chance that the child will be able to develop into a well-adjusted adult.

There will be no need for them to focus on what took place during their childhood, and they will be able to live their life. This is not to say that their childhood was perfect, but it does mean that their needs were generally met.

While this could be described as the ideal scenario, it is not what always takes place; for some, childhood was a time where their needs were rarely, if ever, met, and this may have meant that they felt safer when they were around 'strangers'.

So, even though someone may look like an adult, they might feel like a scared child, and it can then be a challenge for them to experience fulfilment during their adult years. This can, in part, come down to the fact that their childhood left them feeling so empty.

It is highly unlikely that they will be able to simply 'move on' and to put their childhood behind them; there is a strong chance that they will need to re-parent themselves in order to heal the damage that was done by the very people who were supposed to look after them.

To do this kind of work takes great courage, and while it takes time, it will be worth the effort. Something we must remember is that how someone was treated during these years doesn't reflect their inherent worth; the only thing it reflects is what was going on for their caregivers at the time.

One thing that has made it easier for someone to heal from an abusive childhood is the amount of support that is now available, and this is largely due to the internet. Before the internet was available and accessible, people were more likely to suffer in silence.

This is not to say that someone can heal themselves through using the internet alone, but it is a tool that can give them hope and allow them to realise they are not the only ones who had a childhood that was less-than-nurturing. They will have the chance to speak to other people who are in a similar position to them.

On the web, they can discover which books can assist them, and they can find out about support groups and therapists who have the experience to help them. The internet has also allowed people to share their story and to make a difference in the lives of others.

When someone is abused, it is normal for him or her to feel ashamed, and this can stop them from reaching out for the support that they so desperately need. However, in order for them to heal, it is vital that they share their story with people who are able to validate what took place.

As this happens, it will allow them to realise that there is in fact nothing wrong with them, and that the toxic shame they have carried for all these years doesn't belong to them.

Child Abuse – Were You Abused As A Child?

Child Abuse – Were You Abused As A Child?

Why has Child Abuse Gone On for So Long?

In this day and age, it may be hard for someone to comprehend why child abuse has gone on for so long, as well as how this kind of behaviour could still be occurring.

In the United Kingdom, it wasn't until 1986 that a twenty-four hour counselling service was set up to deal with child abuse. This is a free national helpline for children up to the age of nineteen and is called ChildLine.

Prior to that, in 1979, the psychologist Alice Miller released her first book on abuse, titled *The Drama of the Gifted Child*. When this book came out, and for many years after its release, it was met with all kinds of resistance.

This shows that when it comes to awareness of child abuse, it is a relatively new occurrence, and that it is surely a reflection of children finally being seen as more than just 'objects'. For many generations, this was how children were often seen by their caregivers and by society as a whole.

A common saying was 'children should be seen and not heard'. This encompasses the attitude that was so prevalent for many generations, and it is one that was passed on from one generation to another.

Although the saying may not always have been vocalised in its original form, the emotional consequences were often passed on nonetheless.

On top of this was the importance of respecting and honouring one's parents. This could be the idea that the caregiver always knows what's best, or that they always know what's right. For example, there were sayings such as 'don't disagree or argue with your parents'.

Due to the rules above and many others that were similar, it didn't exactly make the child feel that they had a right to speak up or stand up for themselves. Even it something didn't feel right and there was a sense that something was amiss, it would more often than not have been denied and ignored.

This then creates the ideal breeding ground for abuse to be carried out, because if a child is perceived as an object and as something that has no value, it will not be empathised with, or treated with love, care or respect.

As a way to get a child to do as it was told and to create 'discipline', physical punishment was often used, as was mental and emotional forms of punishment. This was partly the result of children being seen as inherently bad and needing to be controlled.

Now, in the current society that we live in, this kind of behaviour is clearly understood as being dysfunctional and – most importantly – abusive. Yet for people who were not brought up with this understanding, what we now call 'child abuse' would in many cases have been accepted as part of the process of both raising and being a child.

This is not only limited to child abuse, however; through the ages, many other things that were acceptable at one point are no longer accepted today, and this is typically due to a shift in people's awareness.

However, in order for this behaviour to be classed as 'normal' and as a way to bring children up, the truth had to remain hidden. This then meant that the child had to deny and repress their suffering and pain.

Due to the pain and the trauma not being allowed to surface, and as the truth of what happened wasn't made known to others, the same style of child rearing was destined to be repeated.

This created an avenue for all of the repressed pain that was never acknowledged or processed to be released onto an innocent child.

As this pain and trauma was never consciously faced with the help of a therapist and/or support group, for example, it is somewhat inevitable that what the caregiver had not dealt with from their own childhood would be projected onto the child.

If the caregiver experienced abuse as a child and has not dealt with it, it is highly unlikely that they will have the empathy or awareness needed to *not* abuse their children – or anyone else for that matter.

But as it was – and still is in some cases – taboo to speak up against one's caregivers who were often seen as perfect and doing all that they could for their children (regardless of whether it was true or not), this original pain would have become trapped in the body.

And whenever someone tries to repress and deny something in order to feel a sense of control, it will ultimately end up controlling them. This is a big reason why child abuse has gone on for so long.

Repression is a common occurrence in today's world, and it can often lead to violence. So, as a society becomes more aware, what is also likely to follow is a reduction in all forms of abuse. The recent changes in society, with regards to child abuse, are a sign that more people are becoming aware.

With a greater focus on child abuse, more can be done to make a difference, and the internet is an incredibly important element to this process, even though it is a fairly recent invention and something that has not been around for very long.

Through using this tool, children can get support that simply wouldn't have been there before, helping them to realise that although it may be normal in their house, it doesn't mean it is right.

Child Abuse – Were You Abused As A Child?

Child Abuse – Were You Abused As A Child?

Chapter One

In the Beginning

Child Abuse – Were You Abused As A Child?

Why are Children Abused?

Abusive parenting is often something that goes on covertly in our society, and to the outsider it might not even be noticed, especially if the caregiver presents themselves to the outside world as the complete opposite of how they are behind closed doors.

These people can hold positions of great responsibility, as well as socially acceptable roles, making them appear to be highly unlikely to be abusive to their child/children. Then there are caregivers who don't hold such high positions, and these are the ones who are often portrayed as more likely to be abusive.

However, it is evident that is doesn't matter what roles someone plays in a society or how acceptable they may appear; people from all backgrounds and walks of life can be abusive.

What is Abusive Parenting?

If someone has been abused, they tend to associate the word 'abuse' with what they themselves experienced. For instance, for some people it might have been physical while for others it might have been emotional.

In any case, what is occurring is that the child's boundaries are not being respected. The child is also being seen as an object and as a possession of the caregiver.

In the book *The Prophet* by Kahlil Gibran, he says: 'they come through you but not from you' (Gibran, 1923). Here he is referring to how children are expressions of life and how they are not owned by the caregiver. This is clearly not the outlook of an abusive caregiver.

Abuse that is carried out on a regular basis can be seen as the worst kind; however, occasional abuse can also be destructive. We are all imperfect human beings who do 'bad' things from time to time, but there is a big difference between the odd behavioural mistake and being abusive.

Responsibility

Children are both vulnerable and dependent on their caregivers; their safety and survival is under their control. As a consequence of this, the caregivers exercise great power and responsibility. The question is: what happens when caregivers are irresponsible and abuse the power that they have?

What is likely to happen is that the children are taken advantage of and are seen as objects for the caregivers to control and to treat however they wish.

The Relationship

These caregivers are likely to position themselves as people to be feared, using different forms of intimidation to control and influence their child/children. As a result, their child/children will not be able to develop a relationship of trust and safety.

This is only normal if a child is never sure what will happen next or how its caregivers will behave. The child can then experience fight, flight or freeze on a regular basis.

Their Childhood

The abusive caregivers are likely to have had a childhood that was just as abusive (if not worse); if someone has experienced abuse, they know how destructive it is and therefore the last thing they should do is carry out the same behaviour, and yet this is often what happens.

Logically this doesn't make sense, and this is because in order to understand the reasons for their behaviour, we have to look at it from another angle.

Ultimately, their behaviour is not conscious and they are unaware of what they are doing, though this is not to say that what they're doing is right. They still carry their pain, and as they have never processed this pain, the abused become the abusers.

Acting Out

So by abusing their child/children, they are acting out this pain, a pain that is years old and that has nothing to do with the children or child involved. Their feelings of anger, revenge and rage – for example – are simply being expressed.

Many years are likely to have passed since they were abused and there are plenty of examples where abused children don't go on to abuse their child/children, due to 'being conscious' of their actions. However, there are also plenty of examples where the same behaviour *is* carried out.

Being Conscious

When different defence mechanisms are in place and someone is no longer aware, it makes it a lot harder to change this dysfunctional behaviour. If years have passed and nothing has changed, it is easy for a human being to become like a robot.

It then becomes extremely difficult for someone to admit to their behaviour and to remove the denial that is often created through years of repression. Having no conscious awareness can lead to a life of reaction, and this is why the less awareness someone has, the more likely it is for them to be abusive.

It could then be said that repression is a precursor to abuse; the more aware and conscious someone is, the less likely they are to abuse another or to abuse themselves.

Why Would a Primary Caregiver be Abusive?

There are, of course, some caregivers who are loving and supportive, and then there are the ones who are anything but.

Instead of doing all they can to create a child who is healthy, happy, empowered and adjusted, they often end up doing the complete opposite. Now, there are of course degrees to how severe this abuse can be, and this will lead to different consequences.

For someone who had loving caregivers that were fairly neutral in this respect, it can be hard to comprehend how someone could abuse their own child, and for someone who was abused as a child, this can also be hard to understand.

Caregivers

Caregivers are often held in high regard by society and rightfully so. However, this has negatives as well as positives. For caregivers who take care of their child or children, this will be well deserved, but when it comes to caregivers who are abusive, it can often create a wall of silence.

The positive perception of what a caregiver is like can cause an abused child or adult to repress and deny what has happened to them.

The Challenge

Instead of them speaking up and being open about their abuse, they may well live in fear of opening up about it. As a result of the common idea of what caregivers are like, it can lead to someone feeling ashamed and guilty of what they actually feel to be the truth within them.

This is why dealing with the consequences of an abusive caregiver, and healing from this trauma, can be such a challenge. As a result of this, the other side of what some caregivers are like often goes unnoticed.

Abusive Caregivers

Ultimately, what's happened has happened, and this means facing the truth of it and not judging oneself in any way; it was not personal and it had nothing to do with the person who was abused. When a caregiver is abusive, it can be a sign that they lack self-awareness.

The abusive caregiver is in pain, and due to them not dealing with their pain in a healthy way, their child ends up being abused. But this is not something that goes on consciously; the whole process can only happen if the caregiver is unaware.

This means that the caregiver's inner experience is creating a sense of unease, and is using the child as a way to regulate their inner processes. Now, these rarely consist of the odd irritation here and there; they are more likely to be extreme and overwhelming to the caregiver.

At times they may be minor experiences within, but in the majority of cases they won't be, and the reason that they are so powerful is typically because they have been building up in the caregiver.

Silence

When the caregiver was a child, they may have also been abused by *their* caregiver, causing them to pass on the same behaviour. Through being unable to speak out about what happened and process what went on, they had to deny it.

This can then lead to repression, and someone can actually forget that they have forgotten. However, the body can't do this; it needs to release what has happened, and if it doesn't get the chance to do that, it can lead to many things including reactive behaviour.

Here someone will behave in ways that are not conscious and they will feel that they have no control. It's as if they have become set to act in certain ways and have no other options to choose from.

The Reminder

Through having a child, all that the caregiver has repressed comes right back up to the surface, and as this pain and trauma has been repressed for many years, it can result in the caregiver having no control over what's going on inside them.

The same behaviour that was carried out on them then gets carried out again, and although this is the case, it doesn't mean that the abusive caregiver will admit to it. Through years of repression and other defence mechanisms — such as justification — the caregiver may have all kinds of reasons to explain why they did it.

Again this will depend on how conscious they are and if they are willing to take responsibility for their actions. One thing is important here and that is — they might deny, justify, ignore or dismiss what happened, but that doesn't mean someone has to do the same thing.

Why Would a Caregiver be Controlling?

The relationship a child has with its primary caregiver is usually the most important relationship they have. This relationship not only plays a massive role in the child's development; it also goes a long way in defining what kind of adult the child will become.

An adult's sense of self, self-worth and their idea of what love is (as well as many other things) are largely the consequence of the relationship they had with their primary caregiver when they were a child. And as the child has come from (through) the caregiver, it is only natural for this relationship to be unlike any other. This is why there can be serious problems in someone's life if this relationship is abusive and/or neglectful.

Controlling Caregivers

When a primary caregiver controls their child, we can see that there is a boundary issue here. The caregiver has no idea where they begin and end and where the child begins and ends, so the child is then perceived as being an extension of the caregiver.

And if the child is an extension of the caregiver and not separate, it is only natural for the child's own needs to be ignored and dismissed.

The Child's Needs

What also happens as a result of this is that the child ends up being enmeshed to the caregiver; the child is then used to fulfil the needs of the caregiver. What is important to the child's development is then overlooked so that the caregiver's own needs are taken care of.

The emotional and mental development of the caregiver may not match their chronological age. Therefore, although the child is clearly a lot younger, when it comes to what is going on at an emotional and mental level, there might not be much difference.

How Does This Look?

There are certain patterns of behaviour involved here, and what usually occurs from this behaviour is that the child is being invalidated and compromised.

The child will usually be treated in a way that says: do what I want and you will be accepted; don't do what I want and you will be rejected and abandoned. The whole idea of unconditional love is nowhere to be found.

Life and Death

At such a young age, the child's whole survival rests in the hands of their primary caregiver, and should the child go against the wishes of the caregiver, it would be tantamount to death. The mere suggestion of rejection or abandonment will be more than enough to control the child.

During this time, it is not possible for the child to question what is going on, as this ability has not yet been developed.

A Disconnection

After the child has undergone many years and many experiences of being invalidated, an inner disconnection is likely to occur. This is the connection the child has with their own inner world, consisting of: needs, wants, feelings and thoughts.

Because of this disconnection, the child is likely to grow up feeling dependent on the caregiver. The child's identity will then not reflect what is true for the child; it will reflect what the caregiver has projected onto the child, including whatever leads to approval.

When the child grows up, it will likely have trouble understanding what's going on inside, and it will be highly likely that they will end up looking towards others when it comes to what to do, what to feel, and how to think.

Why would a Caregiver Control their Child?

There are at least four possible causes here. The caregiver feels powerless; they do not know how to take care of their needs in a functional way; they have poor boundaries, and they feel alone.

It could also be said that all this behaviour (and any kind of abuse) is only possible through a lack of awareness – someone doesn't consciously abuse or take advantage of another.

Powerless

The caregiver controls the child because they feel that they have no control themselves. And because they feel no inner control, they have to control others in order to feel *in* control. Due to the child being weaker and dependent, it cannot defend itself against such behaviour.

Needs

As well as feeling powerless, the caregiver probably feels that they have no way of taking care of their own needs. It is probable that their primary caregiver used them to do the same.

This meant that their needs were denied and neglected, and because they were unaware of this and didn't learn how to take care of these needs, they carried out the same behaviour with their child.

Boundaries

As was mentioned above, because the caregiver has no idea of where they start and where they end, it is not possible for them to notice this in another. And since they cannot see that their child is separate from them, it then becomes normal and natural to see the child as an extension of themselves.

Aloneness

Out of the caregiver's feelings of emptiness and aloneness, they control the child. This means that the child can be used to fill their emptiness.

By the child becoming dependent on the caregiver, they will be unlikely to leave the caregiver. The child will also be used to regulate the caregiver's feeling of aloneness, among other things.

Where did it all Begin?

The caregiver's inner experience may have been carried from one generation to the other.

Child Abuse – Were You Abused As A Child?

Child Abuse – Were You Abused As A Child?

Chapter Two

Generational Abuse

Why Does Abuse get Passed on?

For many years there has been an understanding that child abuse is often passed from one generation to another, and as to how far back some of these cycles of abuse go is anyone's guess.

It is then not surprising for someone to be left confused and astounded at how something so pernicious can be passed on so many times without ever coming to an end.

Change

In order for any kind of change to occur, there has to be awareness. If there is no awareness, then it becomes more or less impossible for change to take place.

And with abuse being so destructive and dysfunctional, it would seem strange that there is often very little awareness around this whole area. What this shows is that either the awareness that the abuser has is not enough, or that the abuser is not aware at all.

How Could This Be?

To say that people who abuse others are unaware might sound incomprehensible. It can be hard to believe that someone could cause another to experience such pain and suffering, all the while being completely oblivious to the consequences of their actions.

Generational Abuse

If someone is not aware of their behaviour or what is going on inside their own mind and body, there is the potential for abuse. Due to a lack of awareness, someone can end up abusing their child/children.

At a surface level it could be said that the reason someone is abusive to their child/children is because they were abused themselves; they are treating them in a similar way to how they were treated.

Repeating the Pain

This is where the confusion can set in. Here we have an individual who was abused themselves, and this means that they also know what it feels like. They have been through the pain and suffering, and yet they are doing to another what was done to them.

This alone makes a human being appear to have no control over their actions. They are not aware; they are being controlled by their childhood experiences.

The Chance to Be Aware

While the above description sounds valid and largely true for people who are abusive, it doesn't answer *why* people are not aware enough to put an end to generational abuse.

Although awareness is part of what can bring abuse to an end, if someone was abused as a child, they are unlikely to have been aware while they were being abused; during the moments of the abuse, there would have been the need to repress and to deny what was going on.

Survival

The reason why the original pain had to be denied and repressed is due to the child's survival resting on its caregivers. At that age, the child has to please the caregivers. If the child was to express how it felt, this could lead to rejection, abandonment, neglect and even punishment.

This whole process will naturally lead to someone having to ignore how they feel. What this will also mean is that someone's ability to be aware of these feelings will begin to diminish at this time.

At this stage, someone's priority is to survive, and the repression and dissociation of their true feelings is often the only way of ensuring this.

Years of Repression

What this does is lay down the early foundations for someone to form a pattern or a habit of continually repressing their original pain and suffering.

However, although it has been pushed down and denied, it still exists in their body. Their inner child will still carry these wounds, and even though they may have grown up and come to believe that they've put the past behind them, this wounded inner child contains the same pain.

More Repression

During these moments of abuse, the child may have been told that it was for their own benefit, that it was what they deserved or that it was for them to learn discipline. What this does is cause the child to believe that what is being done is normal, and that this is how they deserve to be treated.

If this happens – and unless there is someone around to invalidate these messages – the child will grow up to believe what it is being told. This in turn will lead to further denial and repression of how they truly feel.

Blind Spots

What all this repression and denial will do is create blind sports or a lack of awareness of what's going on internally. This means that intellectually, someone may have very little recollection of what happened all those years ago, and while this is true for the mind, it certainly is not true for the body.

The body remembers everything that has happened and contains all of the memories of what took place all those years ago. And as long as what happened in the past remains a mystery and the pain is not faced, they will have very little control over how they express themselves.

The Past Becomes the Present

In order for the abuse to be carried out, these original feelings have to lay dormant and remain out of someone's awareness. As this is the case, they will be continually acted out or acted in. This can then happen through the same or similarly abusive behaviour that was done to them.

Pain

If this original pain is processed with the assistance of another conscious individual, it may enable them to let go and to be free of the past.

The wounded child had to deny and repress what happened in order to survive. This means that this repressed fear of the caregivers can keep them from consciously feeling this original pain.

If it can't be expressed consciously, it will be expressed unconsciously. The first option is functional and will lead to gradual healing, while the second option is dysfunctional and will often lead to further abuse.

Loyalty

What can also play a part in abuse being passed on from one generation to another is the need to be loyal, and this can then cause someone to do to others what was done to them. As a child, someone can take on what their caregivers and ancestors were unable to process, and this is done out of love.

Through being given life, they may have the need to take on what doesn't belong to them as a way to bring balance into the family system. As a result, if one was to put an end to abuse, it could cause them to feel guilty, and as though they are betraying the people who brought them up, as well as the people they have never met.

This is not to say that someone would be aware of their need to be loyal, as this can be something that goes on outside of their awareness. As this need to be loyal continues to exist, the cycle of abuse can continue.

Why Does Neglect get Passed on?

When it comes to what one generation passes onto the next, genetics are at the forefront – some experts say that whatever one generation has, the next are certain to have the same. However, through their understanding of epigenetics, others have said that there needs to be a trigger in order for someone's DNA to have an effect.

This trigger could be an external trigger, such as environmental, or an internal trigger – for example, how someone feels or thinks. What doesn't receive as much exposure as this, however, is how emotional neglect can be passed on from one generation to another.

No Surprise

But, if someone was to step back and look at how the western world is, it is not going to be much of a surprise; this is because the western world and the countries that have been influenced by it are out of balance. The masculine side has been embraced, whereas the feminine side has largely been rejected.

For example, genetics are seen as building blocks and as something that can be changed or removed, just as someone would build a house, create an extension, or remove a part of the existing structure.

Emotions, on the other hand, can't be seen directly but they can be seen through the consequences that they create. It is also not possible to remove them, like someone would move a brick from a house. The masculine approach is about *doing* while the feminine approach is about *being*.

Cut Off

With there being a focus on the masculine and a denial of the feminine, an imbalance has been created, and this means that emotions have largely been ignored.

They are often seen as insignificant and the impact they have ends up being ignored. Someone can't see air, but without it they would suffer, and if this absence lasted for too long, they would die.

The same applies to emotions; they can't be seen and yet they play a big part in someone's life. If they feel good or in balance, certain things will be done; but if they feel bad and are out of balance, it could lead to them behaving in ways that are destructive to themselves and to others.

Childhood Development

Genetics can often be seen as the primary reason as to why someone grows up to be how they are. When this relates to someone's emotional development, it could be said that they feel as they do because it runs in the family. Here they might suffer from depression, have what is often described as an 'addictive personality', and/or have mental problems.

While there may be some truth to this outlook, what it doesn't look into is the kind of care someone received as a baby and a child. The kind of nurturing they did or didn't receive during this time will make a difference to the kind of person they grew up to be.

With the focus being on genetics, its stops attention going where it needs to be. It is through awareness that change takes place; without it, nothing can truly change.

Emotional Neglect

To be neglected during someone's formative years is going to create problems, and the severity of these problems will depend on many different things. For instance, two people could experience neglect and turn out completely different: one person could elevate themselves while another could end up living a life of pain, suffering from their past and even committing suicide.

Firstly, there will be how the neglect affects them and how they respond to these consequences. Then there will be the kind of support that they do or do not receive.

Never Again

No matter what happens after the neglect has taken place and someone becomes an adult, it is likely that they'd promise themselves they wouldn't do this to anyone. However, time passes and someone can end up doing to their own child or children, what was done to them.

As someone suffered so much through being neglected themselves, it can seem strange that they would do the same thing to another.

The Cycle

If someone was to work on their neglect through therapy, or was able to heal it in another way, then the chances of them passing it on are going to be very low. The problems arise when someone is out of touch with what happened all those years ago.

This is a normal response to trauma; disconnecting from what happened is a way to handle the pain. However, although this does allow someone to 'survive', it also means that they are liable to repeat the same pattern all over again.

This is because the pain of what happened has remained within them, and being around a baby or a child that is incredibly needy and dependent can trigger that part of them that feels the same. Because the child then reminds them of this, they will want to avoid the child.

Without Awareness

It would be easy to assume that in order for a caregiver to act this way, they must be 'bad' or 'evil'. However, this behaviour will be a reaction and not something that they have consciously thought about.

When their pain is triggered, the child will be neglected, either through the caregiver physically leaving them or by them being emotionally unavailable. The ability to act consciously is taken away as a result of them carrying so much pain.

Education

This emphasises the importance of education, especially when it comes to the area of emotional development. Emotional neglect can cause someone to be emotionally stuck and so it will be important for them to deal with the pain of what happened – or more to the point, what *didn't* happen – many years ago.

Unless someone wakes up and takes responsibility for their emotional development, there is a strong chance that nothing will change and that the past will be repeated once again.

Child Abuse – Were You Abused As A Child?

Child Abuse – Were You Abused As A Child?

Chapter Three

Denial

Child Abuse – Were You Abused As A Child?

Do You Deny what Happened?

If someone was abused during their childhood, it can be hard for them to think about and admit to what happened.

With what happened all those years ago being repressed to such a degree, an alternate past is able to be constructed; the past can then become the complete opposite to what someone actually experienced all those years ago, at least in their minds.

The Perfect Childhood

Here someone may describe their childhood with great fondness, with all memory of the abuse being denied. Their caregivers might even be admired and idealised.

And because this abuse has not been looked at or processed in any way, it can appear in someone's relationships, behavioural patterns, and in the health of their bodies.

A Disconnection

After each year that has passed, someone can become more and more cut off and estranged from this original abuse. Once this happens, the present difficulties that they experience can appear to be random occurrences as opposed to being a reflection of what happened many years before.

This can then add to the original experience of feeling angry, enraged, powerless, and hopeless. The original trauma is appearing once again and the feelings are the same, but as they are out of touch with what happened, they might not realise what is happening.

Protection

Defence mechanisms are used to protect someone from what the ego mind perceives as a threat, and it is clear to see how this applies to the area of childhood abuse.

At such a young age, someone is vulnerable, powerless, and completely dependent on their caregivers for survival. If these defences were not used, one is unlikely to have made it through all of those traumatic years alive.

Repression

When this abuse is taking place, the child is not being listened to or given the love or mirroring that it needs; it is instead being taken advantage of and being invalidated. As the child is receiving so much negative stimulus, it has two choices.

It can either express how it feels or it can hold onto what it receives. It is unlikely that the child will feel safe enough to express how it feels, given the type of environment that it is in, and therefore it has to push down into the body all that it is feeling and thinking.

The Lie Begins

When the child is being abused, not only does it have to deny, repress, and dissociate from the pain to survive, it also has to deploy these defences when the abuse doesn't take place.

Because although it has all these conflicting messages inside and is also beginning to lose conscious awareness of these, it still has to respond and answer to the caregivers to ensure its own survival.

This could be where someone first loses touch with how they truly feel and what their real needs and wants are. Out of the fear of what their caregivers might do, this truth has to be hidden and will remain unexpressed.

Discipline

The abuse may even be classed and portrayed as discipline, with the idea that the caregivers are only doing it for the benefit of the child. At this age, the child does not have the ability to question what is going on, and as the caregivers are often viewed as god-like figures, there is nothing the child can do. In reality, this is just a cover up, which enables the caregivers to express their own repressed childhood pain.

What then arises in the abused child are the feelings of shame and guilt; this association is formed through how the caregivers respond to the child. If it is being abused, its actions must be bad and therefore the child feels guilty, and as the child is being punished, it feels shamed to the core.

Time Goes By

From the very beginning, the child has learned to survive through repression, denial, and idealising its caregivers. Therefore, unless the child grows up to question what has happened, it is unlikely that these defence mechanisms will ever be removed.

This will not be the easy option, because when questioning or looking over someone's past, there is the potential for extreme pain and trauma to appear again. And without the assistance of a therapist or someone similar, it could cause all kinds of problems should they try to face it alone.

Avoiding Responsibility

Because the caregivers didn't take responsibility for what was going on for them and used their child to regulate their own feelings, the child was made to feel responsible.

The child then ended up carrying all the feelings that they had denied and repressed in themselves. As they could no longer feel them, it was not possible for them to empathise with their child.

Regression

When someone regresses to their inner child and re-experiences all that has not been processed, they will take on the same feelings and behaviours. This will cause someone to feel great pain, and the child's survival will still rest on the caregiver's approval and acceptance.

Someone can then feel as though their survival still depends on their caregivers, with only this inner child knowing who it is in relation to its caregivers.

Do They Deny what Happened?

Caregivers who are abusive can deny that abuse has ever taken place, and if it is not denied, then it may be minimised. Both of these responses can have devastating consequences on the life of someone who was abused.

Denial and Minimisation

Denial and minimisation are defence mechanisms that the ego mind uses, and like any defence mechanism, these are used for protection and stability. The ego mind's main purpose is to keep someone alive; it does not care if something is accurate or inaccurate or whether it is functional or dysfunctional.

Anything that the ego mind perceives as a threat to its own sense of safety and internal equilibrium will be dealt with via a defence mechanism. The saying 'the truth hurts' comes to mind here, and one of the reasons for this is that the ego mind does not run on what is true; its only concern is what is familiar and therefore safe.

Awareness

However, although we have an ego mind, we are not the mind itself; we are the observers of the mind. It is the level of awareness that someone has that will define if it is possible for them to be aware of when these defence mechanisms are being utilised.

When someone has minimal to no awareness, the ego mind becomes like a parasite. Here the ego mind can completely take over, and it will become very difficult for someone to see what is actually going on and therefore take responsibility for it. It is then possible for the past to be completely forgotten – at least consciously – and a kind of amnesia can occur.

Self Regulation

When the abuse was carried out, it allowed the abusive caregiver/s to regulate what was going on internally. The caregivers may have felt angry, frustrated, hopeless, and powerless, and as a way to deal with those painful feelings, they behaved in a certain way toward the child in order to regulate this inner conflict.

And so for the abusive caregiver/s to admit to what happened, they would have to get back in touch with the feelings and thoughts that occurred in the first place. This is likely to be an extremely painful experience, so the defence mechanisms hold the experience at bay.

The Truth Hurts

However, not only would the abusive caregiver/s have to re-experience the feelings that they felt during the abuse of the child; they might also have to experience how they felt during their younger years. If they were also abused, there will be the unprocessed pain and trauma that they experienced as a child.

At first, these defences may have been experienced at certain times, and over the years they would have just got stronger and stronger, until they took over completely. They forget what they have forgotten and then it doesn't matter what is going on externally or what evidence is available.

So Why Does it Matter?

When the child has grown into an adult and no longer needs their abusive caregivers to survive, it can seem strange that there would still be any tension or that they would still be affected.

The reason for this is that although someone may have grown physically, their emotional development is likely to have been inhibited through what happened. On one side, there is the abuse that will cause problems for the child when it grows up, and on the other side there is the invalidation of what happened.

The pain of the past will be trapped in someone's body, and they will continue to experience the same feelings, thoughts, and sensations until this pain has been looked at and processed. The reason for this is due to the repression that occurred, and nothing ever changes by repressing it; this only leads to more problems.

Inner Child

When these past experiences have not been looked at, someone is at the risk of regressing to their inner child, and with a history of abuse that has not been looked at, it is unlikely that their inner child is going to be in a good way.

Their inner child will be attached to the abusive caregiver/s out of the need to survive. It will then need the approval, acceptance, validation, and attention of the abusive caregiver. So the very things that the inner child needs from the abusive caregiver/s is something that was never given by them all those years ago, and there is the chance that it may never be given by them at all.

Child Abuse – Were You Abused As A Child?

Do Other People Deny that You Were Abused?

When someone has been abused as a child, they have already gone through enough, without having to prolong the pain of what happened. However, what can add to this pain is when someone finds that the people around them don't believe them.

Their need to be heard and validated for what they have gone through is then not going to take place. Instead, they can be told that they are lying, exaggerating what happened, and remembering events that didn't take place, amongst other things.

They then don't receive what they need to receive and can be made to feel as though they are the problem. The person or people who were abusive can end up looking innocent, and although the person in question was abused, they can feel as though they are in the wrong.

Self-Doubt

One response to this is that someone can end up doubting themselves and wondering if they are making it all up. They might wonder if the people around them are right, thinking they may be out of touch with what actually took place.

But no matter what the people around them say, they are not going to be able to change what happened. It won't matter what other people believe or even if they begin to doubt themselves, as the truth of what happened is still within them.

Vulnerable

Through being abused, there is the chance that they still feel vulnerable, and this can make it even harder for them to stand their ground. They could be in a position where they are still dependent on the people around them, due to their age, their financial situation, or many other reasons.

If they haven't had the chance to open up to anyone about what took place and to get the assistance they need, they could be carrying a lot of trauma with them. It could then be a challenge for them to speak their truth and let other people know what really happened.

Survival

Because of what happened to them, there is a strong chance that their sense of safety has been compromised. This could mean that their ability to feel safe in their body, and the knowledge that they deserve to exist, has been affected.

Therefore, they might find that they have the tendency to go along with what other people say, regardless of how true it is. Based on the abuse that they experienced, pleasing others might be what feels comfortable, while expressing their truth might feel uncomfortable.

Trapped

To open up about what happened is not always easy, and it is going to be a lot harder when the external support is not there. This could cause someone to feel trapped; making them believe there is no way out.

When the people that someone is closest to (or the people who they expect to support them) end up turning their backs on them, it can be hard to understand and accept. This is why therapists and support groups can be so important.

What's going on?

When someone opens up about what has happened — or what might still be happening — and comes up against a wall of resistance, it can come as a surprise. The other person could disagree with them, ignore them, or even walk away. In some cases, it could lead to even more abuse, and they could then end up being re-traumatised.

However, while this can cause someone to feel even worse — believing that they deserved to be abused or that there is no hope — it is not about them. They are likely to be in a position where they need to be reassured and are therefore vulnerable, but how other people respond is not personal.

The Other Person

When they tell someone they were abused, it could be someone the other person knows, or it could be someone they don't know — either way can play a part in how they respond. If it is someone the other person knows, they might not believe what they say as a way to protect the image or idea they have of the other person.

Cognitive Dissonance

If they were to embrace what they were being told, it could create an inner conflict or what is described as 'cognitive dissonance'. Here, the other person would be forced to question how they see the other person, something that could be too painful for them.

They would have to let go of how they saw the other person, and this would be experienced as a form of loss. The person is still alive, but how they view them is no longer accurate. So, if they maintain the idea they have of the other person, they won't have to experience pain.

Avoidance

Another reason why someone might not be believed is because of what it might trigger in the other person if they were to accept what is being said. This can relate to both someone who knows the abuser and to someone who doesn't.

As it is not uncommon for abuse to occur, there is the chance that the other person could also have been abused. However, while the first person is aware of what took place and is looking for support, the other person may have disconnected from what took place in their own life.

As they are out of touch with what happened, they are not going to want to place their attention on anything that would remind them of it. If they were to do that, it might cause all the pain that they have repressed to come to the surface, so instead they choose not to believe.

Living a Lie

This person then is an example of how they would be if they disconnected from what happened and gave off the impression that everything was fine. It is not always easy for someone to embrace how they feel, especially when it relates to the people or person who brought them up. Disconnecting from what happened might have been the only option the other person had.

Do You Idealise your Caregivers?

Although there is no such thing as a perfect childhood, that doesn't mean that everyone is treated in the same way. There are people who were treated well on most occasions, and then there are others who had the opposite experience.

In this case, someone would have been treated badly on most occasions and this is what was normal for them. There is also the chance that someone had a certain stage in their childhood where they were mistreated.

Perhaps someone experienced some kind of abuse and/or they may have been neglected. When it comes to abuse, it is going to relate to what someone received from the people around them. On the other hand, when it applies to neglect, it is going to relate to what they *didn't* receive.

Different Ways

Then there is what takes place when someone receives something that harms them, and what takes place when they don't get what they need to receive in order to grow and develop. Each form of abuse is destructive, and while it will affect people in different ways, there will be certain consequences that generally arise.

As a child, someone may have played up and got themselves into trouble as a way to get their caregivers' attention, and although they might not have received the attention they wanted, it would have been better than being ignored.

Pain

If someone was abused, the ideal situation would be for them to reach out for support and to gradually process their emotional pain, but this is often the exception as opposed to the rule. This is partly due to the fact that in today's world, emotional pain is generally overlooked.

During someone's time in the education system, they would have been given the chance to develop their mind and to learn about their body. Yet the same can't be said when it comes to someone's emotions; this is an area that is often ignored.

The Mind

If it was a case of just getting in touch with the pain, processing it, and then moving on, it would be relatively straightforward, but someone's mind can end up getting in the way, stopping them from getting in touch with how they feel in their body. This pain can then be projected onto others.

How someone feels in their body is going to be different to what is taking place in their mind, and in order to avoid the pain in their body, someone may have created all kinds of stories in their mind. Some may even have created a whole a new identity for themselves.

Idealisation

The idea someone then has of their caregiver/s can be out of touch with the reality of what they were really like (and are still like). During the time of the abuse, it would have been vital for them to idealise their caregiver/s.

At this age, a person's survival depends upon their caregiver/s, meaning that they would have had to block out anything that put their survival at risk. If they were to face reality, it would be overwhelming and too much for them to handle at this age.

Time Goes By

However, just because someone is an adult it doesn't mean they feel like one, and this can cause them to maintain the idealised image that they created as a child. While this stops them from having to face how they felt all those years ago, it won't allow them to move on from what happened.

Two Sides

When someone sees their caregivers as perfect, it allows them to experience a certain amount of control when it comes to how they feel – this is the upside. The downside is that someone will be living in denial, and their relationships and/or their body will show them exactly what is going on within them.

If someone was to drop their idealised image, they would open themselves up to how they really feel, and this could be too overwhelming (just as it would have been as a child).

Chapter Four

The Consequences

Child Abuse – Were You Abused As A Child?

Do You Feel like there is Something Wrong with You?

If someone has experienced some kind of abuse during their childhood, they can come to the conclusion that there is something inherently wrong with them, and if they were violated by someone whom they looked to for protection, love, and support, it is not going to be much of a surprise.

Two Ways

There are at least two ways that someone can believe they are flawed. The first is through their own interpretations of what they experienced, and the other is through the words their caregiver/s – or the other people around them at the time – used.

At such as young age, they are completely dependent on their caregivers, meaning that their survival rests upon them. Therefore, they have to maintain an idealised image of them even when reality doesn't match it; to see them for who they really are would create all kinds of inner unrest and anxiety.

The Problem

This is partly why someone will see themselves as being the problem, rather than their caregivers. Another reason is that at a young age, they will see themselves as the centre of the universe, with everything therefore being taken personally.

At such a young age, they are not going to have had the ability to question what took place, but that doesn't mean that it felt right, or that every part of their being would have accepted what happened.

Unquestioned

They could experience conflict over what happened and question what took place, or they could be defined by it. Either way, their life is being shaped in one way or another by this deep wound. Toxic shame is going to be one of the emotions that emanates from the wound within them.

Projection

No matter what someone had to put up with or go through, it had nothing to do with their inherent worth as a human being – instead, it had everything to do with the mental and emotional state of their caregiver/s.

What was going on with them internally defined what they saw externally, so all they ended up seeing was what they were not prepared to face within themselves. Their true value was then covered up, as a result of another person's lack of awareness and inability to take responsibility for their own pain.

Inherent Worth

But although someone might have lost contact with their true worth, it has always been there and it will never leave them.

What are the Effects of Having a Caregiver who was Verbally Abusive?

From the moment someone is born, their caregivers have an incredible power over them; they have the power to build them up or the power to tear them down. Ideally, someone's caregivers would have been loving, supportive, and kind, but this doesn't always happen.

They could have had a caregiver who wasn't nurturing on the odd occasion, or they may have always been this way. And as they have so much power, it won't necessarily matter whether someone had a caregiver who was verbally abusive every now and then, or all the time.

Damage

The fact that they have been exposed to this kind of behaviour – no matter how often it occurred – is enough to cause all kinds of damage, and while they may no longer be a child, it doesn't mean that the past is truly behind them.

There is the chance that their caregiver is still causing them problems, and yet they don't need to be in contact with them for the problems to still be there. They could have passed away or they could have cut off all contact, but their presence can still remain, and this is because they can still exist in their mind.

The Taboo

However, even though they had or still have a caregiver who is verbally abusive, it doesn't mean that they are able to admit to how they truly feel. One of the reasons for this is because of how caregivers are generally portrayed by society.

Amongst other things, they are generally seen as people who deserve to be revered for the effort they put into raising a child, and this is an outlook that will apply to a lot of caregivers out there, but as anyone who has been verbally abused by their caregiver will know – it doesn't apply to all of them.

This social conditioning – along with the views of other people who had loving caregivers – can stop someone from facing their emotional truth. Should someone face how they feel, they could end up feeling guilty, ashamed, and fearful, as well as having to experience being rejected and abandoned once more.

Denial

These factors can then cause someone to live in denial, and the longer they live this way, the longer it will take them to truly heal themselves – if they ever do. They will continue to be tormented internally and be attracted to situations that mirror what is taking place within them.

If someone denies how they feel, they can end up blaming their caregiver for what happened. This may allow someone to experience a momentary release, but it won't allow them to move on from what occurred.

Wide Open

As children, some people wouldn't have had any boundaries, and so they would have been wide open to all that was said to them. If someone had a caregiver who generally gave them massages that were positive, supportive, and empowering, this wouldn't have mattered.

The problems would have arisen when someone had a caregiver who was critical, hateful, and abusive, as this is what the child would have internalised. Everything would have been taken personally, even though it was simply an expression of the pain that their caregiver was in.

Ultimately, it would have had nothing to do with who someone was, and yet that wouldn't have mattered; it came from their caregiver, and so it was taken as the truth.

Self-Image

As these messages entered someone's mind, they would have gone on to become their self-image. So their views of how worthy they are, their value, how competent they are and how lovable, can depend on how they were treated.

When it comes to people who were verbally abused by a caregiver, there is going to be the chance that their self-image is not very empowering or even very accurate. They might feel as though they are unlovable, a failure, and that no matter what they do in their lives, they will never be good enough.

Inner Voice

How they talk to themselves may also have been defined by how their caregiver spoke to them. In the beginning, their caregiver would have needed to be around for them to be verbally abused, but as time passed, their voice would have become internalised.

This voice – as well as their self-image – can cause someone to sabotage their relationships, their success, their happiness and their health. Instead of them being their own best friend, they can be their own worst enemy.

What are the Effects of Having a Primary Caregiver who was Emotionally Unavailable?

It is relatively easy for physical abuse to be noticed, as there is the chance that there will be external evidence (that is, unless someone is able to cover up the marks). Emotional neglect, on the other hand, is not as easy to notice, and this is due to the fact that there is unlikely to be any physical marks.

However, if someone is aware of how someone can react as a result of experiencing neglect, they might be able to notice what is taking place. This can apply to both a child who is currently being neglected and to an adult who is suffering from the consequences of being neglected as a child.

Neglect

A child can be neglected as a result of their primary caregiver leaving them, but their caregiver can also neglect them while being in the same room; the defining factor is whether they are emotionally available or not. This could be because someone's caregiver is caught up in their work, has mental and emotional problems, or perhaps because they have experienced a loss in their life and are unable to be emotionally present.

If the caregiver ended up being emotionally unavailable later in life, it might not cause as much damage as it would have done if they were emotionally unavailable in the beginning of someone's life. This is because they are likely to be stronger as the years go by, and this inner strength wouldn't have been developed before.

Invisible

In order for someone to develop a sense of self, and to therefore be in touch with their needs, feelings, and personal power, as well as knowing where they begin and end, they will have needed to have had an empathetic caregiver. This would have been someone who validated their feelings and needs, something that would have allowed them to develop boundaries and a sense of personal power.

Yet, if someone's caregiver was not emotionally available, there is still the chance that their sense of self didn't develop. What is likely to have developed is a false-self, and this would have been what allowed them to survive. Their true-self ends up not being able to see the light of day, and they are therefore likely to feel invisible.

Consequences

Although now an adult, their emotional development is unlikely to match up, making them feel like a baby or a child. They could have trouble knowing what their needs are, as well as what they're feeling in each moment.

If they were then to get in touch with their feelings, they could experience incredible rage, and this can be the result of them being ignored by their caregiver. Along with rage, they could also experience the following feelings: rejection, abandonment, toxic shame, fear, hopelessness, helplessness, guilt, and grief.

It's Safe

What happened during these early years is going to be something that they want to put behind them, but they could find that the people they are attracted to remind them of their caregiver. This is partly because what happened during these early years would have ended up being associated with what is safe.

The people in their life no doubt look different (although they might have a physical resemblance), but they end up feeling and thinking the same. This is therefore going to mean that they could behave in the same way, and they could also find that they only feel safe when they avoid attention.

What are the Effects of Being Invalidated as a Child?

During someone's early years, it would have been important for them to have been validated by their caregivers. This is not to say that they had to be validated at all times, but it is something that would need to have happened consistently.

If this didn't occur, it could be due to a number of reasons, one of them being the result of abuse taking place. Invalidation may then have been something that happened every now and then, or it could have occurred on a regular basis.

But as everyone is different and doesn't necessarily respond in the same way, it may not have needed to happen all the time; it may have caused problems even if it happened on the odd occasion.

Of course, the fact that it happened at all could have been enough to harm their mental, emotional, and physical growth, stopping them from forming a healthy sense of self.

Validation

When someone is validated as a child, both their inner and outer worlds are acknowledged. This can include their feelings, thoughts, views, experiences, ideas, senses, perceptions, wants, and needs, amongst others things.

All of these elements come together to form their sense of self, their boundaries, and their experience of life. Having an external influence – such as the primary caregiver – validating these aspects means that it would enable them to develop in a myriad of ways.

Development

Their brain would have developed through this taking place; it would have allowed them to know that they exist and that they are worthy of love and life itself. What they experience internally (feelings, thoughts, and needs) and what they experience externally (perceptions, experiences, and observations) can then be trusted and accepted as being real.

As Time Passes

They would have gradually learnt to navigate their way through life and to build trust not only in themselves, but also in other people. Another important occurrence here is that through the primary caregiver validating and regulating what they were feeling, it would enable them to develop the ability to emotionally regulate themselves.

The need to repress and deny their emotions during these years (and then as an adult) is unlikely to exist – at least in most cases. This can mean that they won't grow up to feel emotionally numb, overwhelmed, or weighed down by their emotions, and neither should they vent them through violence or destructive behaviours.

The Real World

However, this doesn't always occur; if it did, the world would be a very different place. The above may have happened during the odd occasion.

When the complete opposite of the above happens, it will be classed as abuse. When this occurs, what they experienced – both internally and externally – would have been either denied or ignored in some way.

Invalidation

As a result, their sense of self is unlikely to develop, and they can start doubting their thoughts, feelings, needs, wants, and perceptions. It can then seem normal for them to question their existence, to ponder whether they are worthy of love, or if they can trust their own judgements or those of other people. Boundaries will then have to give way and be replaced by walls, or they could end up being enmeshed to others.

This can also stop their brain from developing as it should. For example, they may not have learnt how to navigate their way through life, simply because inner and outer trust was not allowed to form. Their needs and wants can also be a mystery, as a result of their caregiver ignoring and denying them, while using them to fulfil their own needs and wants.

Emotional Pain

This is all going to create a lot of emotional pain and trauma that they may disconnect from in order to survive. The primary caregiver is likely to have been emotionally unavailable, and therefore didn't have the ability to assist them in regulating their emotions so that they could develop the ability themselves.

As an adult, they may have to carry a lot of emotional pain around and could end up feeling overwhelmed and weighed down by their emotions and life in general. They could feel emotionally trapped and may not even know that life could be any different. If they don't harm themselves through holding the pain within them, it may end up being acted out, resulting in them harming others.

Is Having Boundary Problems Normal?

Boundaries are a vital part of life, and are essential when it comes to someone forming healthy relationships, moderating their experience of life, and being able to feel safe enough to show their true-self, amongst other things.

They allow a person to know where they begin and where they end, as well as where other people begin and where they end. Without them, a person can feel invisible, vulnerable, unsafe, sensitive, and empty.

Boundaries help people feel safe to be themselves, and allow them to have their own personal space. This person can say yes to people, but most importantly – they can say no.

Abuse

Although it is important for a person to have boundaries, child abuse generally doesn't allow people to develop them. The main reason for this is that the abusers don't have any either.

They don't understand that their child/children are separate beings and that they have their own personal space. This does not register in their minds; therefore, violating a child is normal to them.

If they had boundaries, they would be able to see that what appears to be coming from the child is actually what is going on within themselves, but due to a lack of awareness, it can seem as though the child is the cause of their inner tension.

No Choice

This can only lead to problems, with the child having no way of protecting itself. At such a young age, they have no boundaries and they are not aware of their sense of individuality. The child therefore has no other choice than to put up with this kind of behaviour.

They are dependent, meaning that they can't say 'stop' – or if they do, it is unlikely to be heard. At this age, it will often come across as normal, and as something they deserve. They will simply believe this is what love is.

Consequences

Through someone having to put up with this kind of behaviour as a child, it doesn't enable them to realise that they have their own personal space, or that this is something that is sacred and needs to be protected.

A person can have no idea where they begin or end or where others begin and end. To be violated, compromised, and taken advantage of, can then feel normal and just how life is. That someone has the right to not only say yes, but also no, may not even be known to them.

For people who have boundaries, saying no or maintaining their personal space will be a natural thing to do and generally won't cause them to experience fear, but to people who don't have boundaries, it could lead to intense fear being triggered if they were to stand up for themselves.

Pain

To stand up for themselves and to have boundaries might lead to someone feeling that they could be rejected, abandoned, attacked, humiliated, and ignored.

Do You Tolerate Unhealthy Relationships?

When someone experiences some kind of abuse in their adult relationships, they may say that it is a reflection of what took place during their childhood, or they could come to the conclusion that their childhood was fine and that it has nothing to do with it.

In the first example, there is no doubt whatsoever about where this abuse was first experienced. As they are certain about it, they can take the steps to deal with what is taking place.

When it comes to the second example, the whole thing could come across as a mystery, not making any sense to them. This could cause them to feel like a victim, or perhaps that they are just unlucky.

Healing

The first person might then decide to look at their history, their intention being to heal themselves. How long this takes can depend on how severe their early abuse was, and on the kind of support they receive, amongst other things.

Through knowing where the abuse originally came from, they will have a target, something to aim for. Knowing where to look and the kind of questions to ask will enable someone to take action.

Complete Honesty

This will also mean that they will need to be completely honest with themselves. For instance, there could be guilt, toxic shame, and fear that could stop them from being able to admit to what happened.

It can be easy for someone to have an idealised image of their caregivers or the other figures around at the time, and this can sabotage the whole process, primarily because this will stop someone from embracing the truth and this truth will need to be faced in order for someone to heal themselves.

The Unknown Cause

When a person comes to the conclusion that their childhood was fine, a different approach will be needed. Someone might believe that they have no control over who they attract or the kind of people they are attracted to, with attraction simply being a random process.

If they are relatively young, they might come to the conclusion that they will grow out of it and that this is just part of growing up. The opposite sex could also be labelled as being a certain way – for example, that all men/women are the same and can't be trusted.

It could also be put down to them just having low self-esteem and confidence issues. So, through building themselves up, they will be able to move beyond this challenge, with very little being mentioned about their childhood and what kind of effect this had on them.

The Next Stage

Someone could end one relationship that is abusive and attract another person who is completely different, with that being the end of it. It would then appear as though they have experienced an internal shift.

They could, of course, experience the same thing over and over again, ending up confused, frustrated, angry, and powerless. They then feel stuck, and unable to attract the kind of person who will treat them in the right way.

A Closer Look

However, just because someone was abused during their childhood, it doesn't mean that they can remember it or even want to admit to it. It could also be something that hasn't been recognised as abuse, something that was seen as normal in their family of origin.

This means that someone could be in denial, and could have cut off all recollection of their childhood (or just certain parts) in order to avoid feeling the pain of what took place. While this allows their mind to maintain their childhood illusions, their body and the people they attract will tell the real story.

Normal

They also don't need to be someone who experienced extreme abuse during their childhood in order to attract abusive people in their later years. All that needs to take place is for someone to experience a one-off violation or something that compromised them in one way or another.

This can then create an opening, and through this, there is a chance that it will get bigger and bigger. What first started off as being fairly insignificant can go on to become something far worse.

This could have been a caregiver who was critical and controlling, or it could have been a caregiver who was overprotective and who got too close.

Tolerance

What these early experiences do is create a tolerance to that kind of behaviour, as it is familiar to them. A person can then be drawn to people who remind them of their caregivers.

It won't matter if this is something that will enhance their life or not. Someone might consciously feel repelled by certain behaviour, and yet unconsciously, they could feel drawn towards it.

Another person might start off being overprotective or slightly controlling in the beginning, but as time passes, this can gradually increase to include abuse that is far worse. The original experiences may have made them receptive to this kind of behaviour.

Child Abuse – Were You Abused As A Child?

Chapter Five

Moving Forward

Do You Need to Forgive Them?

When it comes to moving on from an abusive past, it is not uncommon for someone to hear that they need to forgive; the act of forgiveness is highly regarded by many people and numerous schools of thought.

Intellectually

On an intellectual level, forgiveness sounds like a good idea, as it is something that is morally right. Here someone can come to the conclusion that to do anything other than to forgive would create further problems and yet more pain.

Based on the recommendations of others and on how someone perceives the past, they may want to forgive and move on, and perhaps for some people, this process does work.

Two Options

This leaves people with two options: either they can go down the intellectual route and forgive their caregiver/s, or they can avoid all talk of forgiveness and remain immersed in the pain that is a product of their childhood.

At this point, the first option is going to sound better: who would want to be constantly stuck in their past, if they could just forgive their caregivers and move on? It sounds like the logical option, and to be the one of reason.

A Metaphor

One way to describe this scenario is to imagine that a house has been destroyed. There is debris everywhere, and no matter where the owner looks, there is work to be done. This can lead the owner to two conclusions: he can either ignore the problem and abandon the house, or he can try to rebuild the house from the ruins.

To the owner there are no other options; all he sees are these two choices. If the owner were to avoid the problem, it would be similar to intellectualising, and to try to rebuild it from the ruins would be analogous to being trapped by the past. He hasn't thought about removing the debris and starting again.

Two Sides of the Same Coin

On the surface, forgiveness sounds like a terrific idea, as opposed to being constantly affected by the past and living a life that's a walking nightmare, a Hell on Earth.

If we look at this from a deeper level, however, we can see that these are actually two sides of the same coin. What happened all those years ago had consequences, and these consequences produced internal debris. Just like in the metaphor above, the debris has to be dealt with before anything else can be done.

What happened all those years ago will not simply disappear as a result of some logical or moral conclusion, and being constantly overwhelmed by what happened is not the answer either.

Facing the Truth

What needs to occur is the complete acknowledgment of what happened all those years ago, but this is not the same as being overwhelmed by what happened – as someone would be in their day-to-day life or their earlier experiences.

This can involve being with an individual who is aware enough to allow someone to express and feel all that they were not allowed to feel as a child. This needs to be done without the judgement of what is right and wrong, and what should or shouldn't be felt.

How Is This Different?

The reason this is different to the other two options is because in both of those choices, someone is identifying with their past. This means that the person is holding onto the past.

Out of this attachment to the past, the person is either running away from it — through intellectualising about what happened and forgiving — or they are being constantly exposed to what happened by regressing to those past experiences.

The Forgiveness Trap

One of the reasons forgiveness appears to be such an attractive option is because it can allow someone to avoid what is taking place within them. Due to the original abuse that took place, a person can fear their caregiver/s, and these fears will have been repressed and pushed out of conscious awareness.

This means that whenever someone goes to express these original feelings, these fears will appear and they can be overwhelmed by them. Here someone will regress to the hopeless and dependent child that they once were.

Ruled By The Past

Most people will want to avoid this so they don't have to re-experience those original feelings. Therefore, the intellectual standpoint of forgiveness can allow someone to avoid feeling the original wrath of their caregivers.

When someone regresses to their wounded inner child, they will embody the child's needs once more. This child needs to be approved and accepted, and forgiveness can allow this to happen.

Is Forgiveness Important?

It could be said that it is not about either forgiving or not forgiving someone's caregivers; what is important is to be honest with oneself and to allow these original feelings to be processed.

Is it Important to be Angry about what Happened?

One emotion that someone will have experienced when they were abused is that of anger, but while they will have felt it at certain points when growing up, it doesn't mean that they've stayed in contact with it.

This could be an emotion that they were not allowed to show as a child, and although time has passed, they may have continued to cover up their anger as an adult. Or they could be someone who is constantly angry and unable to feel any different.

Safe

Whether someone is cut off from their anger or consumed by it can be the result of what felt safe during their early years. To express anger at this time might have lead to more abuse, and to cover it up may have minimised how much they had to suffer.

On the other hand, a person could have been protected by their anger, having been able to avoid more abuse by being angry. This could have been how things always were, or perhaps they switched between the two, depending on what was taking place.

Violation

But as they were violated in one way or another, anger, as well as rage, is to be expected. These emotions are there to inform a person that their personal space is being infringed upon, and that some kind of action needs to be taken.

The trouble is that at such a young age, they are limited in what they can do. They are completely dependent and vulnerable, as well as not having the physical strength to stand up for themselves.

If they didn't feel safe, they would have had to disconnect from their anger. Instead, they might have ended up feeling fear and anxiety, with this being a pattern that has stayed with them into adulthood.

One Consequence

They can also end up becoming someone who is never too far away from being angry, and while this might stop them from being abused as an adult, it could also cause them to abuse others.

The smallest thing could remind them of what happened all those years ago, making them into the perpetrators. The cycle of abuse continues, and the person is nothing more than a slave to their emotions.

They are in touch with their anger, and while that can be a good thing, they can also become possessed by it. Anger is then not something that aids them; it is something that has the potential to destroy them, as well as others.

Another Consequence

Alternatively, they could be someone who has lost all contact with their anger, meaning that they are nothing more than a doormat, with them being walked over and abused by others on a regular basis.

They might pride themselves on never getting angry, and this could be part of their identity, but while going to the other extreme is destructive, being completely cut off from this part of themselves is no better; while it might mean that other people are not harmed, it could mean that someone is harming themselves.

Benefits

Many years ago this would have been what kept them safe and therefore alive, and yet as an adult, this is going to cause them problems. These early experiences would have made someone tolerant to abuse and comfortable with being treated badly.

Deep down, someone might even believe that they deserved to be treated in the ways that they were, with toxic shame, guilt, and fear being the emotions that stop them from being angry about what happened.

Change

However, in order for change to take place, they will need to get out of their passive state and get uncomfortable with what happened – and what might still be happening to them. The reality is that they did not deserve to be abused, and they have every right to be angry.

Anger will allow them to feel powerful; however, this doesn't mean being consumed by it and using it to harm others. It will be important for them to contain their anger and use it to move forward in order to put an end to their suffering.

Moving Forward

Through being angry, a person can go to the next stage, and this can be what they need in order to process the anger and the rage that they are experiencing. This step can include feelings such as abandonment, rejection, powerlessness, hopelessness, and grief.

Someone may need to seek the assistance of a therapist and/or a support group. Controlled anger won't solve everything, but it will get the ball moving.

Is Feeling Safe an Important Part of Healing?

When someone is abused as a child, there is the chance that they are going to have trouble feeling safe in the future. This would have been something that they first experienced when they were growing up, and something that has stayed with them throughout their adult years.

For some people, it will be easy to match their current experience with what happened many years ago. They will be aware of what took place, and because of this it will be clear as to why they currently feel as they do.

However, in some cases, someone might find it hard to feel safe as an adult and have absolutely no idea why this is. Their body is then unable to relax and to feel at ease, but their mind has no insight into why this is.

Normal

While this may seem strange – especially if someone was abused as a child – it is actually normal. When someone experiences something that is painful or traumatic, the mind can end up blocking it out as a way to ensure their survival.

If someone was a small child when they were abused, they would have needed to deal with the pain somehow; if no one else was around to stand up for them or to comfort them, then there wouldn't have been any other option.

Conditioning

Time will have passed, and this means that their mind will have become conditioned over the years. These original experiences that remain in someone's body will then be overlooked by their mind, but this is not the only thing that can cause someone to become disconnected from their body.

When it Happened

When a person is abused by someone they look to for their own survival, there is the chance that they will have to hide their true feelings. It is not going to be safe for them to express them: this could cause them to be harmed even more, or to be neglected.

Two Sides

What this can mean is that someone can find it hard to feel safe internally due to what happened on the one hand, while on the other hand they might find that the conditioning they received on top of this pain stops them from seeking the assistance they so desperately need.

This will be a challenge that someone is faced with after they have been able to get through their mind and into their body. When someone is caught up in their mind and out of touch with what their body is telling them, they might just feel unsafe without knowing why.

The Mind

In order for someone to process what is going on in their body, they will have to deal with the obstacles that the mind will create. For example, this may relate to an idealised image that they have of their abuser/s, with this image stopping them from having to face their emotional truth.

Someone might also wonder what the other people in their family will think if they were to reveal what happened. Guilt, toxic shame, and fear can also arise and make them question if they are doing the right thing, stopping them from going any further.

The Body

However, no matter what someone's mind is saying, it is their body that needs to be listened to; their body knows what happened all those years ago, and this won't change just because the mind doesn't want to face the pain, or because it has been conditioned to believe something else.

However, if someone doesn't feel safe, then they are not going to be able to embrace the truth of what happened, and telling oneself that they need to feel safe and/or trying to force it is unlikely to work either.

Feeling Safe

In order for someone to open up, they will need to feel that it is safe for them to do so, and when they experience this on the outside, they might be able to experience it on the inside. At the same time, being in an environment that is safe might not be enough.

This is why the assistance of a therapist and/or support group is so important in this process. Of course if someone doesn't feel safe on the inside, it might not matter how safe their external environment is, as their inner experience can end up being projected onto others.

Moving Forward

By finding a therapist that a person feels comfortable with, it will give them the chance to work through what is in their body. It could take a while for them to build up their trust, but as time passes, they may gradually open up.

Is Being Validated an Important Part of Healing?

When someone is abused as a child, they can grow up to believe that they deserved what happened to them, and how they end up feeling – as a result of what took place – can start to become normal.

It then doesn't stand out and is not recognised as something that doesn't reflect their true-self. There is also the chance that someone has questioned what took place.

Reasons

One reason someone wouldn't know that how they felt wasn't the truth is because they wouldn't have experienced anything different. If they were violated in some way when they were growing up and they hadn't come across anything that went against what happened, then this would be taken as the truth.

If someone has questioned what happened – even if only partly – they will have come across something or someone that shows that how they were treated was not personal. Of course, at the time it might have felt personal, as they wouldn't have had the ability to know any different.

Alternate Point of View

Someone may have had a family member around at the time who treated them differently, giving them another way of looking at themselves. But if someone didn't have this and the only feedback they got was that they were 'bad' or 'worthless', for instance, then it can be a lot harder to question what happened.

As A Child

As time passed and the abuse continued, a person would have had no other choice than to accept it. However, this doesn't mean that it would remove all resistance, or that every part of them would be in agreement with how they were treated.

A Seed

Similar to how a seed will grow into a plant or a tree over time, this inner resistance may start to grow stronger. This might not be a smooth process, however, as although someone might not like how they feel, it may have become familiar and what they are used to.

If they keep going, they will gradually start to come across people and information that make them see things differently. These sources will give them new insights into what happened, and allow them to connect to that part of them that always knew something wasn't quite right.

Hidden Wounds

After being abused by a caregiver who they looked upon for love and protection, it can be a challenge for someone to completely embrace the fact that they didn't deserve to be treated as they were.

Deep emotional wounds will have been created, and even though time has passed, these can still define how they feel about themselves and about life. And, as child abuse can be dismissed and denied by other people, as well as making them feel ashamed of what happened, it can be a challenge for them to open up about what took place.

Validation

Someone could come across another person who treats them differently, or read about something that goes into what they experienced, and their whole world could begin to open up. It is then no longer just something they have always felt within them; it is something that many others have also gone through.

How they have felt for their whole life is then partly or completely explained – they are not going mad and there is nothing inherently wrong with them; they have simply been doing their best to cope with a dysfunctional upbringing.

Someone can then understand that based on what happened, how they feel and how they behave is normal and to be expected, and that anyone else could end up feeling the same if they went through the same experiences.

Moving Forward

A therapist can make such a difference – providing that they are trained in this area and therefore don't invalidate someone's experience. They can allow someone to open up about what happened, without them fearing that they are going to be invalidated, ignored, or shut down.

Someone might have had to wait a long time to receive this validation, but it doesn't mean that it is too late for them to get it. There will no longer be the need for them to deny how they truly feel, and they will no longer need to carry the emotional baggage of their past around with them.

Is Crying an Important Part of Healing from Abuse?

Because of the bond that someone can have with their caregivers, it has been said that more damage can occur when someone is abused by a family member than when they are abused by someone who is a family friend or a stranger.

Resilience

How someone responds to the abuse, and what happens as the years go by, can depend on their level of resilience. It could be said that some people are more robust than others, and this is naturally going to affect how they respond.

Another thing that can define how resilient someone is – and therefore how they respond – is at what age they experienced the abuse. If it took place after their first few years, that person is going to be a lot stronger than if they experienced it at the beginning of their life.

Neglect

As a baby, someone may have been neglected or experienced another type of abuse, and this would have put them on the back foot to begin with. This could then mean that they are not as resilient as they would have been if their needs had been met during this incredibly important developmental stage.

Someone may have continued to be neglected as time went by, and this would have meant that they didn't have any corrective experiences. Their external environment remained the same and so they continued to suffer as the years went by.

Enlightened Witness

Another thing that can make a difference here is if there was anyone else around at the time who showed them that not everyone is the same. Alice Miller described this person as an 'enlightened witness', and they would have shown them love and kindness, among other things.

This position could have been filled by another family member, or it could have been a teacher, a family friend, or a mentor. What this shows is how much of a difference one single person can make, and how someone can either lift another up or pull them down.

The Next Step

However, no matter how resilient someone is or whether they had people around them who were different, they are still going to be carrying pain. The years they spent being in an abusive environment would have left a mark on their mind and body.

This varies from person to person, as not everyone is going to be affected in the same way, yet this pain is going to need to be faced in order for the abused to liberate themselves from what happened.

The Conscious Approach

When someone faces their pain, they are taking their power back, and this is also going to benefit the people around them. For example, the whole time this pain remains within them, it can come out in the form of reactive or unconscious behaviour.

Although someone can be disconnected from how they felt as a child, it doesn't mean that this pain has disappeared; the body's natural response is to push out what doesn't belong there – this is one of the reasons why spots appear. Therefore, it is important for someone to consciously face their pain as opposed to allowing their pain to control them.

Avoidance

It is human nature to avoid pain, meaning that a person can end up doing everything they can to avoid what they're feeling. How they feel as a result of not getting their needs met can end up defining their life.

There are two sides to this pain, though: on one side is the rage that someone will have experienced, and on the other is the sense of being helpless. One side is going to make someone feel strong, and the other is going to make them feel weak.

Unmet Childhood Needs

If someone was to identity with the rage that they experienced, there is the chance that they will do to others what was done to them. This is a form of indirect revenge and takes place when someone is consumed by their emotions.

Alternatively, if someone goes beyond the rage and embraces how they feel underneath, they will be taking responsibility for how they feel and they will be able to let go of what has built up in their body. Here, the person will get in touch with their unmet needs, something that is likely to be painful.

Moving Forward

When it comes to grieving their unmet childhood needs, they may be able to cry out the pain by themselves. However, in the beginning, they will probably need assistance.

This is something that can be provided by a therapist and/or some kind of support group. Through this support, someone will go where they wouldn't have gone before, and they will also provide the positive regard that they need in order to heal.

Loyalty

If someone finds that they only get so far by working through their emotions, it could be a sign that they are holding onto the past out of their need to be loyal to their caregiver/s. In this case, the child part of them won't allow them to move forward; to do this would cause them to feel guilty, as though they were betraying the people who gave them life.

As a child, someone may have taken on what their family and their ancestors were unable to process. It might then be necessary for them to have a family constellation in order to let go of these entanglements.

Acknowledgments

I would like to thank the authors who have made a difference to my life with their writings, as well as the other people I've met who have also had an impact on my life.

While there were moments where I received support that I'd been actively looking for, there were also moments where this support seemed to come out of nowhere, and in each case, the support came when I needed it the most.

Thank you to my late father for showing me his kindness and humanity. You allowed me to see that not everyone is the same, and that what I have to say matters.

My only wish is that you were here for longer, but I knew it was time for you to go. You had been through enough, and I hope you are now at peace.

I would also like to thank Sheila Baynham and Ian Baillie for their support and encouragement.

And thank you to all of the friends who have been there for me throughout my life. I appreciate your time and support.

Child Abuse – Were You Abused As A Child?

About The Author

In 2003, Oliver JR Cooper began the journey of wanting to know who he was, and of understanding what life was all about. He read vast amounts of psychological books, took courses, and actively worked on his own transformational healing.

Keeping a journal to track his progress of insight and discovery, Oliver felt compelled to share this information with others who were also seeking an effective means of internal transformation. In five years, Oliver has written over 840 articles that have garnered over 524,000 click-throughs so far.

His Topic Genres include: Abuse, Behaviour, Boundaries, Defence Mechanisms, Emotional Intelligence, Happiness, Men's Psychology, Movie Metaphors, Relationships, Self-Image, Self-Realisation, Social Causes, The Ego Mind, and Women's Psychology.

Oliver JR Cooper also offers transformational coaching.

To find out more about Oliver, please go to:

www.oliverjrcooper.co.uk